LIVING IN THE WILD: BIG CATS

Charlotte Guillain

Heinemann
LIBRARY

Chicago, Illinois

© 2014 Heinemann Library
an imprint of Capstone Global Library, LLC
Chicago, Illinois

To contact Capstone Global Library please phone 800-747-4992, or visit our website www.capstonepub.com

Edited by Clare Lewis and Adrian Vigliano
Designed by Tim Bond
Original illustrations © HL Studios
Picture research by Tracy Cummins
Originated by Capstone Global Library Ltd
Printed in CTPS

17 16 15 14 13
10 9 8 7 6 5 4 3 2 1

Library of Congress Cataloging-in-Publication Data

Guillain, Charlotte, author.
 Jaguars / Charlotte Guillain.
   pages cm.—(Living in the wild. Big cats)
 Summary: "Here's an animal lover's one-stop source for in-depth information on jaguars! What do they eat? How do they behave? Are they
at risk? This book also includes loads of fun and fascinating facts about
dolphins, as well as maps, charts, and wonderful photographs of these
clever creatures."—Provided by publisher.
 Includes bibliographical references and index.
 ISBN 978-1-4329-8106-8 (hb)—ISBN 978-1-4329-8113-6 (pb) 1.
Jaguar—Juvenile literature. I. Title.

 QL737.C23G847 2014
 599.75'5—dc23   2013013022

Acknowledgments

The author and publisher are grateful to the following for permission to reproduce copyright material:
AP Photo p. 25 (Milwaukee County Zoo); Getty Images pp. 11 (Tom Brakefield), 16 (Suzi Eszterhas), 17 (Carol Farneti-Foster), 20 (SA Team/ Foto Natura), 22 (Brian Mckay Photography), 33 (Panoramic Images), 35, 45 (Mint Images - Frans Lanting), 37 (José Enrique Molina), 43 (Gerry Ellis); National Geographic Stock pp. 23, 31 (SA TEAM/ FOTO NATURA/ MINDEN PIC), 29 (FRANS LANTING), 39 (STEVE WINTER); Nature Picture Library p. 19 (Luiz Claudio Marigo); Newscom p. 41 (EPA/Francisco Guasco); Shutterstock pp. 6 (Matt Gibson), 7 (Ewan Chesser), 9 (Hedrus), 12, 15 (Pal Teravagimov), 18 (TOMO); Superstock pp. 5 (Minden Pictures), 13 (NHPA), 24, 27 (Gerard Lacz / age footstock), 34 (age footstock).

Cover photograph of a jaguar reproduced with permission of Getty Images (Mint Images - Frans Lanting).

We would like to thank Michael Bright for his invaluable help in the preparation of this book.

Every effort has been made to contact copyright holders of any material reproduced in this book. Any omissions will be rectified in subsequent printings if notice is given to the publisher.

Disclaimer

All the Internet addresses (URLs) given in this book were valid at the time of going to press. However, due to the dynamic nature of the Internet, some addresses may have changed, or sites may have changed or ceased to exist since publication. While the author and publisher regret any inconvenience this may cause readers, no responsibility for any such changes can be accepted by either the author or the publisher.

Contents

Some words are shown in bold, **like this**. You can find out what they mean by looking in the glossary.

What Are Big Cats?

A shadow moves through the trees of a tropical forest. It moves silently towards an unsuspecting deer, getting closer and closer. Suddenly the dark shape leaps out and seizes the deer in a deadly bite. This powerful killer is a jaguar.

Jaguars are mammals that are included in a group called big cats. The term "big cat" has different meanings, but generally refers to the larger wild cats, such as jaguars, lions, tigers, leopards, pumas, cheetahs, snow leopards, and clouded leopards. Sometimes the term big cat is used more specifically to include the larger cats that can roar. These are jaguars, lions, tigers, and leopards only.

As well as being able to roar, this smaller group of big cats shares the following features:

- They are all above a certain size.
- They are all carnivores.
- They are all **apex predators**. This means no other animal hunts them for food.

BIG CAT NAME

The word "jaguar" comes from an American Indian word, *yaguará*. This is thought to mean "large beast of **prey**" or possibly "he who kills with one leap."

Jaguars spend a lot of time around or in water.

Big cats live in different parts of the world in a range of **habitats**. These include the grasslands of Africa, the forests of North America, the mountains of Southeast Asia, and the swamplands of South America. Some, such as tigers and jaguars, are good swimmers. Some, such as pumas and leopards, live alone, while lions live in large groups called prides. All big cats have colored or pattered coats that help to conceal them as they hunt prey.

What Are Jaguars?

The jaguar is one of the largest, most powerful big cats and is the biggest cat in North and South America. A jaguar has a similar coat to a leopard, with golden-brownish fur patterned with dark spots, called **rosettes**. Sometimes the spots on a jaguar's back blend together to look like a stripe. This fearsome hunter has a strong, sturdy, muscular body, with a large head and powerful jaws. Jaguars can vary in size according to where they live, but the males are always much larger than the females. A male jaguar can weigh as much as 350 pounds (160 kilograms), while the heaviest females weigh about 187 pounds (85 kilograms).

Black panthers

Some jaguars and leopards have completely black fur and are often called black panthers. Animals that have black fur rather than the typical coloring for their **species** are described as **melanistic**. A change in their **genes** has made this happen. Scientists think the black fur helps to **camouflage** the jaguar in darker places and so it has become a useful **adaptation** for survival.

A female jaguar can have some cubs with patterned coats and some with black fur in the same **litter**.

SPECIAL SPOTS

In the same way that every human has a unique set of fingerprints, the rosettes on a jaguar's coat are in a different pattern for every individual. This helps scientists studying jaguars to identify different cats and monitor population numbers. A jaguar's rosettes are different than a leopard's as they have a dot or dots in the middle, while a leopard's do not.

How Are Jaguars Classified?

All living things are put into groups, or **classified**, by scientists. This helps to identify every living thing accurately and to explain how and why they live where they do. Classification means grouping living things according to the features that they share.

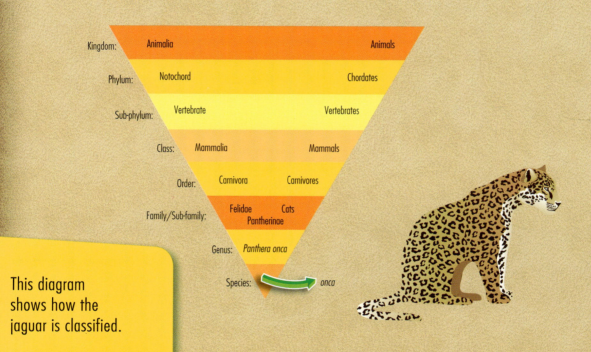

Kingdom:	Animalia	Animals
Phylum:	Notochord	Chordates
Sub-phylum:	Vertebrate	Vertebrates
Class:	Mammalia	Mammals
Order:	Carnivora	Carnivores
Family/Sub-family:	Felidae / Pantherinae	Cats
Genus:	*Panthera onca*	
Species:	*onca*	

This diagram shows how the jaguar is classified.

Classification groups

Classification triangles are used to show how each living thing is classified. Towards the bottom of the triangle each group contains fewer and fewer members. For example, there are fewer animals in the order Carnivora (carnivores) than there are in the class Mammalia (mammals), and so on.

Jaguars are in the family Felidae, which includes all cats, large and small, wild and domesticated.

Special cats

Living things are given a scientific name, such as *Panthera onca*, so they have a single name rather than many different names in different languages. Sometimes living things are grouped into subspecies within a species because of small differences between them. There are no subspecies of jaguar but their size varies in different regions.

Leopards look similar to jaguars but have longer bodies and are slimmer and lighter.

Where Do Jaguars Live?

All wild animals live in a habitat. This is the place where an animal can find everything it needs to live, such as food, water, and shelter. Jaguars live in a range of habitats, such as dense forests, grasslands, swamps, and even deserts. They tend to live where there is plenty of water, either near rivers or streams or in swampland. Jaguars can live as far north as the southern United States. Today they are mostly found in remote parts of Central and South America, ranging from Mexico to the north of Argentina. The biggest population of jaguars lives in the vast Amazon rainforest.

Use this map to see where jaguars live around the world.

A perfect jaguar habitat has plenty of water, thick vegetation, and lots of animals to hunt.

A place to hunt

Jaguars live in habitats where they are able to hunt and kill plenty of prey. When jaguars hunt, they stay on the ground and like to have plenty of cover from plants and trees to help them stalk prey unseen. They also like to climb into trees to locate prey or hide.

HIDDEN CAMERAS

Scientists in Arizona have set up cameras in a mountainous region that have captured recent photographs of jaguars. Jaguars used to live in New Mexico and Texas, as well as Arizona, but during the 20th century these populations disappeared. Now it is thought that a few cats have moved back to Arizona from Mexico. Scientists hope that these cats might **mate** and the population could grow again.

What Adaptations Help Jaguars Survive?

Animals have adaptations that help them to survive in their particular habitat in a particular way. These adaptations develop in a species over thousands of years. Jaguars are adapted to be able to hunt prey successfully in the habitats where they live.

Camouflage

The rosette patterns on a jaguar's fur are an important adaptation for this stealthy predator. Hiding is important because a jaguar hunts its prey by stalking and ambushing rather than chasing over long distances. On the forest floor, the dappled light shining down through the trees blends in perfectly with the pattern on a jaguar's coat, helping to camouflage it. In more open terrain the pattern also acts as camouflage by breaking up the animal's outline. Jaguars with black fur are well camouflaged in dark, shadowy places.

Jaguars need to stay hidden for as long as possible to get close to prey animals.

Swimming

Unlike many other cats, jaguars are adapted to be able to swim very well. Their strong, sturdy legs and large paws enable them to do this. These adaptations give the jaguar more choice of prey, as it is able to hunt for turtles, fish, and caiman in rivers as well as stalking animals on land.

HUNTED

Like many other big cats, in the past the jaguar was hunted for its beautiful coat. During the 20th century, as many as 18,000 jaguars were killed every year to make fur coats and other goods for humans. In 1973 this fur trade was virtually stopped and today selling parts of a jaguar's body is against the law.

Jaguars can climb trees while hunting prey or looking for a place to rest.

Night vision

Like many other cats, jaguars have eyes that are well adapted to hunting for prey at night. Many animals that have good night vision have a structure at the back of their eyes called the tapetum lucidum that acts like a mirror. This reflects any light giving the animal much clearer vision than an animal without this adaptation. Jaguars have this special eye adaptation. A jaguar's eyes are positioned at the front of its face, giving it **binocular vision**. This enables them to judge distances well, which helps them decide when to leap out at prey.

Other senses

A jaguar's sense of hearing is also adapted to help it locate prey. Its small, rounded ears are very sensitive and can turn in the direction of any noise they pick up. This helps the jaguar to assess where prey is very accurately. They can even turn their ears in separate directions at the same time.

A jaguar's sense of smell is well developed but it tends to use this to find other jaguars to mate with rather than to track prey.

WHISKERS

Jaguars have a set of sensitive whiskers around their face and head, with most around their mouth. These whiskers are called vibrissae and work by gathering information from the movement of air near the jaguar, telling the hunter if prey is nearby. A jaguar relies especially on its vibrissae when hunting in the dark. Its whiskers are also **tactile**, playing an important part in the jaguar's sense of touch.

A jaguar's eyes are positioned at the front of its face. This is one feature that helps make them excellent hunters.

Jaguar jaws are the strongest of all the cats.

Killer jaws

A jaguar's stocky head contains a set of large, powerful jaws. The jaguar's huge jaw muscles define the shape of its face. This adaptation enables the jaguar to hunt and kill almost any other animal in its environment. A predator with such powerful jaws has no problem crunching through the skull of its prey after it has leapt in for the kill.

The huge canine teeth inside the jaguar's mouth help it to grip hold of struggling prey and to tear flesh from its victims as it feeds. The jaguar is the only cat that uses its canine teeth to bite between its prey's ears and pierce its brain to kill it.

Strong body

Jaguars also have powerful, muscular bodies. They need this strength to hold down prey and to drag it to a better location to feed on once killed. A jaguar's stocky legs and body make it easier for the cat to creep low to the ground as it stalks its victims. Its short, muscular legs enable it to leap from a standstill, while its strong front paws are useful for climbing trees.

MOVING JAGUARS

Jaguars as we know them today have been around for between 280,000 and 510,000 years. They used to live much further north, but scientists believe they moved south as the climate became colder. Having made their home in warmer climates, the jaguar then developed various adaptations over time that suited their new home.

Jaguars can even crack open the tough shells of turtles with their powerful jaws.

What Do Jaguars Eat?

Jaguars are carnivores and only eat meat. Because jaguars live in a range of different habitats, their diet can vary considerably from place to place. Like many other cats, jaguars are **opportunistic** hunters, which means they will eat many different types of animals should they come across them. Eating a wide range of species is very useful, because if one type of animal is affected by changes in the environment, there should still be plenty of other prey animals left for the jaguar to eat.

Varied diet

Scientists studying jaguars in the wild have counted more than 85 species eaten by them. The animals they tend to eat most often include capybara, a large mammal that looks a bit like a big guinea pig, and peccary, a pig-like mammal. Other common prey are birds, deer, armadillos, tapirs, and domestic cattle. Jaguars will also hunt for food in water and so their diet includes fish, turtles, and caiman, an alligator-like reptile.

Capybaras live in groups and spend a lot of time in water.

Hunting

Jaguars creep up close to prey before leaping out and surprising it. The jaguar then makes a swift kill by biting through the victim's skull or clamping its jaws around its prey's throat to suffocate it. It can kill smaller prey with one swipe of a front paw. Jaguars can also leap into water to catch prey. They are strong swimmers, so can carry prey back to the shore before eating.

JAGUAR ATTACKS

Jaguars do not normally attack humans. They tend to keep out of people's way and will only hurt humans if they are cornered or wounded. Unfortunately, in many places where jaguars live people are afraid of them and may shoot the cats to avoid attack.

Feeding

A jaguar tends to eat large prey starting at the head, eating the tongue and then internal organs. When eating a turtle, the jaguar will either break open the shell with its teeth and jaws or scoop out the turtle's soft body from under the shell with its paw. Jaguars need to eat at least 3.1 pounds (1.4 kilograms) of meat each day on average to get the energy they need.

Jaguar food web

All animals have to eat plants or other animals to live and they, in turn, may be eaten by other animals. This is called a **food chain**. The energy in a food chain starts with the sun. Plants use the sun's energy to make food and are called **producers**. Animals are called **consumers** because they consume (eat) plants or other animals. Animals that eat plants for energy make up the next link in the food chain. These include many of the animals eaten by jaguars. Carnivores make up the next link in the food chain, getting their energy from the animals they eat. Many connected food chains make up a **food web**.

Jaguars can eat extra meat when they kill large prey and then go several days without eating.

CARLOS A. LOPEZ GONZALEZ

Carlos A. Lopez Gonzalez is a Mexican scientist who has studied jaguars in the wild. He has observed jaguars to monitor whether prey of a certain size was important in their diet. His research concluded that jaguars don't depend on large prey, such as peccaries, but survive just as well on a diet of medium-sized prey.

This is a food web. The arrows go from the plant or animal being eaten to the animal that eats it. In this food web capybaras, peccaries, and fish eat plants. Jaguars eat capybaras, peccaries, and fish. They also eat the caiman that eat the fish.

Jaguar

Caiman

Capybara

Fish

Peccary

Rainforest plants

River plants

What Is a Jaguar's Life Cycle?

An animal's life cycle is the stages it goes through from birth to death. A jaguar's life cycle goes through three main stages: birth, youth, and adulthood. Jaguars reach adulthood when they are old enough to **reproduce** and have cubs themselves.

Meeting and mating

Adult jaguars usually live and hunt alone, apart from mothers caring for cubs. Jaguars can mate at any time of year but the best time to have cubs is during the rainy season as there is much more prey around. Female jaguars are normally about two to three years old when they mate, while males tend to be three to four years old. The females attract a mate by making special sounds at certain times of day and **scent-marking** her territory. Once they have mated, the male and female separate and live alone once more.

Adult male and female jaguars only spend time together when it is time to mate.

22

A newborn jaguar cub weighs about 8 times as much as a newborn pet kitten.

Birth of cubs

A female jaguar is **pregnant** for about 100 days. She finds a safe and sheltered place to give birth, in a den located in a cave or under a fallen tree trunk. She can give birth to between one and four cubs, but usually has two. Newborn cubs weigh about 28.9 ounces (820 grams).

RAINFOREST SEASONS

The jaguar mostly lives in tropical regions, which have two seasons: a rainy season and a dry season. The rainy season lasts for several months, with heavy rainfall and hot, humid weather. During this season there is an increase in plant growth, making more food at the start of the food chain.

Cub development

Jaguar cubs are born with their eyes closed. They only open them after around two weeks. They are completely dependent on their mother; feeding on milk produced by her and staying safe in the den for several months. They are able to start walking after about 18 days. Cubs start to eat meat as well as drinking milk after about three months. Initially, this meat is brought to the den by their mother. Cubs continue to drink milk until they are about six months old.

Jaguar cubs learn to play with each other and their mother when they are small.

Staying safe

Mother jaguars are very protective of their cubs. Young jaguars could be attacked by harpy eagles or by adult males that kill them off to reduce competition. This is why the cubs stay safe in their den until they are old and strong enough to run away from danger and learn from their mother.

SPECIAL CUBS

In November 2012, two jaguar cubs were born at the Milwaukee County Zoo in Wisconsin. Conservationists think these cubs are extra special because their father was born in the wild. He was killing cattle and so was taken into captivity for his own safety, bringing new genes into the population of captive jaguars. Both cubs are male and so will be much needed when they mature to mate with the mainly female population of jaguars in zoos. Breeding programs in zoos and other institutions are important for keeping up the numbers of species that are endangered in the wild.

GENTLE JAWS

Like many other cats, a mother jaguar carries her cubs in her mouth. She might do this if she senses danger and needs to move them to a new den. She is able to hold her cubs gently in her lethal jaws without hurting them.

Learning to hunt

When jaguar cubs are around six months old, they are old enough to leave the den and go out hunting with their mother. This is important as they gradually learn how to hunt by watching her. Playing and wrestling with siblings and their mother is also an important part of learning to hunt for a predator.

Independence

Jaguar cubs leave their mother at around two years of age but they may keep in touch from time to time for several months after this. When the cubs reach the age of three or four years, they are ready to mate themselves and the cycle will begin again.

CUBS IN CAPTIVITY

Most of what we know about jaguar cubs has been learned by scientists studying their development in captivity. Jaguars are so rare and their young cubs are so well-hidden in the wild that it is hard for scientists to monitor them in their natural habitat.

A jaguar cub stays close to its mother until it is old enough to survive on its own.

Cat	Lifespan in the wild
Cheetah	around 12 years
Lion	around 15 years
Jaguar	around 15 years
Leopard	around 15 years
Puma	around 20 years
Tiger	around 20 years

This chart shows the lifespan of some big cats in the wild.

How Do Jaguars Behave?

Jaguars tend to live alone, except when mating or raising cubs. Like many other predators, jaguars are **territorial**. This means they mark out their own area of land, called a **home range**, and defend it against other jaguars. Doing this ensures there is enough prey available for them to hunt and eat when they need to.

A female jaguar needs to be able to hunt over an area of about 9.5 to 14.6 square miles (25 to 38 square kilometers), while males need two or three times as much space. Two or three females might have their home ranges within one male's home range. Some home ranges have been observed to be over 100 square miles. Jaguars will spend a lot of time traveling within their home range every day.

Defending territory

Male jaguars can defend their home ranges in two ways: by fighting other males that intrude and by marking their space. However, scientists studying jaguars in Brazil have observed that male jaguars there were not particularly aggressive towards other males entering their home range. They are more likely to mark their home range by making noises, scratching bark off trees at the borders of their territory, scraping the ground with their back feet, and by scent marking plants using **urine** and **feces**.

WILD SECRETS

It's difficult for scientists to gather information about jaguars' behavior in the wild, as they tend to live in remote habitats with dense vegetation. Knowledge about jaguars' behavior has mainly been pieced together by putting radio or GPS collars on cats, studying photographs taken by **camera traps**, and observing the presence of tracks and kills.

Scratching bark off of trees is one way male jaguars mark their home range.

Hunting and resting

Radio collars fitted to jaguars have shown scientists that jaguars can be active at any time of day or night, probably depending on the activity of prey where they live. Like many other big cats, their preferred time for hunting is early morning and early evening. This behavior is known as **crepuscular**. When the day is particularly hot, from mid-morning until mid-afternoon, jaguars tend to rest. They find a secluded spot deep in the shade, for example under rocks, inside caves, or under leafy plants and trees. Sometimes they climb trees to rest on a strong branch.

Strong swimmers

Jaguars love water and will often stay close to it as they move around. In the Amazon rainforest, jaguars rarely stray further than one third of a mile from water. They enjoy swimming and can use rivers to travel to islands where prey might be found. Jaguars swim with their head and back above the waterline and will even play in the water as cubs.

JAGUAR CAMP

The Jaguar Research Center is located in the Pantanal tropical-wetland region in Brazil and provides a unique opportunity for people to observe jaguar behavior. Visitors can stay at the camp and are almost guaranteed a sighting of jaguars, as so many live in that particular area. They can be seen catching prey in the river and resting in the shade. Most scientific observations of wild jaguar behavior have been made here.

Jaguars use water to cool off when temperatures become very hot.

A DAY IN THE LIFE OF A JAGUAR

A jaguar's day consists of sleeping, resting, and hunting. A female jaguar in the wild might sleep from midnight until around 3:00 am. She would then wake up and start to roam around her territory, hunting for prey. After making a kill in the early morning, she will take her victim to a safe place to feed herself. Then she takes some meat back to her cubs in their den and also feeds them with milk.

During the hottest part of the day a female jaguar often rests in the shade with her cubs, **grooming** them by licking their fur with her long tongue. She will also spend a lot of time grooming herself, particularly her forelegs and paws. Cubs enjoy playing and wrestling with each other and their mother. The family might visit the river to cool down and play some more. The mother jaguar is careful to get her cubs back to the safety of the den or to a new den if she senses a male jaguar is nearby.

As dusk falls, jaguars that have not already hunted that day will search for prey before stalking it and killing it. As night draws in they will sleep again, either in their den with cubs or in a high place, such up a tree or on a rock.

LEANDRO SILVEIRA AND ANAH JACOMO

Leandro Silveira and Anah Jacomo are Brazilian biologists who cared for three jaguar cubs after their mother was shot by cattle ranchers. Leandro and Anah taught the cubs how to hunt, climb trees, and swim so that eventually they might be able to survive in the wild. After two years, the scientists tried to release the jaguars but when the cats roamed close to farmland they had to be taken back into captivity for their own safety.

It's important for jaguars and other big cats to rest during the day to save energy for hunting.

How Intelligent Are Jaguars?

It is difficult to identify and measure what we know as intelligence in animals. Much of the way they behave is based on **instinct** as much as intelligence. However, jaguars seem to demonstrate intelligent behavior in several ways that are crucial to their survival.

Communication

The way animals communicate tells us a lot about their intelligence. Jaguars communicate in a variety of ways, mainly using sounds and smell. Jaguars can make a range of noises, including roaring, which is mainly used to warn intruders to leave another cat's territory. They make a grunting sound that is a bit like a cough to communicate with other jaguars over a long distance or to mark out their territory. Jaguars can also make a snorting, or chuffing, noise that is known as prusten. This is a friendly noise that is similar to the purring sound made by other cats. Tigers, snow leopards, and clouded leopard can also make this noise. Jaguars use prusten when they are relaxed and contented.

Jaguars are also able to use their sense of smell to interpret markings left by other jaguars. These include scraped up earth, urine sprayed into bushes, and feces left in prominent places. These markings tell them if they are entering another jaguar's home range.

A jaguar's roar sounds like a deep, loud cough.

JAGUAR TALES

Stories told by South American Indians have described jaguars that dip their tails into rivers to lure fish to the surface so they can catch them. If this were true it would mean jaguars are able to use a "tool" (their tail) to help them catch prey. However, there is no evidence to prove this behavior so we can't be sure that it really happens.

What Threats Do Jaguars Face?

Jaguars face a number of threats which have led to them becoming a species in danger. The Convention of International Trade in Endangered Species (CITES) is an organization that registers animal population numbers to alert governments, conservationists, and the public if a species is decreasing in numbers. CITES has classified jaguars as "near threatened."

Loss of habitat

A major threat to jaguars is loss of their habitat, mainly due to forest being cut down by humans to use the land for farming and the wood for building. Jaguars need to be able to roam over long distances within a region ranging from Mexico to Argentina, but human development often stops them from moving where they want to go and makes it difficult for them to find a mate.

This map shows the past and present ranges of the jaguar.

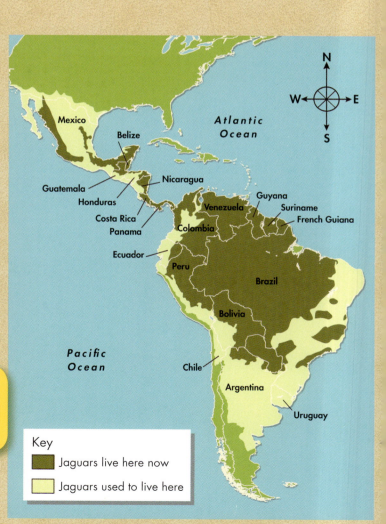

Key
- Jaguars live here now
- Jaguars used to live here

Loss of prey

Although jaguars will hunt a wide range of prey animals, it is becoming harder for them to hunt. There is less prey available in the reduced space left for them after habitat destruction. Humans also hunt the jaguars' typical prey, leaving fewer animals for the cats to feed on.

Human threat

The expansion of the human population is one of the biggest threats to jaguars and many other wild animals. When jaguars move into areas where people live and farm to search for prey, they are likely to kill farm animals, which makes them very unpopular. Very often jaguars are shot by ranchers, who see jaguars as a threat to their livestock. If a mother with cubs is shot then the young jaguars usually die too.

How Can People Help Jaguars?

Many people and organizations are working hard to help protect jaguars. This beautiful, mysterious animal appeals to many visitors in zoos and wildlife parks around the world. In zoos, endangered species such as the jaguar can be studied, so we are able to learn more about their needs and behavior. Captive jaguars can also take part in breeding programs that help to boost population numbers. Visitors to zoos and wildlife parks learn about these stunning creatures and are more likely to support any efforts to protect them in the wild.

JAGUAR HUNTING

The fur trade used to be responsible for the deaths of thousands of jaguars each year. This trade has now been made illegal, but jaguars are still shot by people who either ignore laws protecting them or have permission to kill the cats. Animals that cause a problem to farmers can still be hunted in Brazil, Peru, Costa Rica, Guatemala, and Mexico. In Bolivia, hunters can get permission to kill jaguars as **trophies** and in Ecuador and Guyana jaguars are completely unprotected. Jaguars are now extinct in El Salvador and Uruguay.

This scientist has put a radio collar on a jaguar so its movements can be followed.

Protected areas

In order for populations to increase, jaguars need to live in special areas where they are not under threat from humans. In Belize, a wildlife preserve has been set up to protect jaguars. 58 square miles (150 square kilometers) of rainforest has been made into a reserve, where around 200 jaguars live. In Brazil a special center is to be set up to focus on the conservation of predators such as the jaguar and to work with farmers and other people who can come into conflict with the cats.

Conservation groups

As well as governments in Central and South America, conservation organizations are working hard to protect jaguars. These include the World Wildlife Foundation, Panthera, and Jaguar Conservation Fund. They raise awareness about these and other endangered animals and raise money to help protect them.

Panthera has taken a leading role in jaguar conservation. It was involved in setting up the Jaguar Preserve in Belize and is currently involved in the Jaguar Corridor Initiative (JCI). This initiative involves 13 of the 18 countries where jaguars live. Because there are no subspecies of jaguar, this big cat is the same wherever it lives. It is the only large carnivore of this type in the world that moves over long distances and so the JCI is an attempt to create a "corridor," linking jaguars from Argentina to Mexico, so the animals can roam as far and as freely as they need to. Working with governments and other charities, the JCI works with local communities to help them live alongside jaguars and farm cattle without coming into conflict with the cats.

Eco-tourism

People who live in areas where jaguars are found can benefit from the income brought by eco-tourism. This involves visitors staying locally in order to visit the jaguar's habitat and see them in the wild. The benefits of eco-tourism act as incentive for humans who share space with jaguars to help protect them.

These jaguar cubs were born at a zoo in Mexico in 2012.

DR. ALAN RABINOWITZ

Dr. Alan Rabinowitz is CEO of Panthera and a big cat expert. During the 1980s, he was involved in the first radio-collaring of jaguars in Belize and went on to play an important role in the setting up of the country's jaguar preserve. The Jaguar Corridor Initiative is one of Dr. Rabinowitz's greatest achievements. He has also worked on a similar corridor initiative for tigers in the Himalayas.

What Does the Future Hold for Jaguars?

The jaguar isn't as endangered as many of the world's other big cats, but it still remains "near threatened." Although laws have been passed to protect this magnificent cat, unless they are enforced effectively, jaguar numbers will continue to fall as they are killed in great numbers or lose more of their habitat.

Governments need to ban jaguar hunting altogether and instead focus on educating the people who live alongside jaguars to help them understand what a valuable species it is. If the jaguar is protected and able to flourish then many other species that share its habitat will be protected too.

Positive steps

Activities to protect jaguars, such as the Brazilian government's National Center for Research, Management, and Conservation of Predators and the Jaguar Corridor Initiative, should go a long way towards addressing the threats jaguars face. If everyone is committed to understanding and helping jaguars, then we can hope that they have a future in the wild.

JAGUAR PROTECTION

The Wildlife Conservation Society (WCS) began a jaguar conservation program in 1999, focusing on scientific research into jaguars' needs. They work to protect jaguars in areas where their populations are dwindling, showing farmers that using guard dogs can protect their livestock from jaguars so they don't need to shoot them. They also look at environmentally friendly ways to keep jaguars away from human settlements and reduce pollution that can harm the cats.

This jaguar lives in a zoo in Belize.

Jaguar Profile

Species:	Jaguar
Latin name:	*Panthera onca*
Length:	4 feet (1.2 meters)
Weight:	220–350 (100–160 kilograms)
Tail Length:	2–3 feet (60–90 centimeters)
Habitat:	Dense forests, grasslands, swamps, and deserts in Central and South America
Diet:	Capybara, peccary, birds, deer, armadillo, tapir, domestic cattle, fish, turtles, and caiman, among other animals
Number of cubs per litter:	Around one to four cubs, with two on average. Females are around two to three years old when they are ready to have cubs and give birth about once every two or three years.
Life expectancy:	Up to 15 years

The spotted coat provides good camouflage for hunting.

Large eyes are able to see well in the dark and judge distances accurately.

Short, strong back legs help the jaguar creep close to the forest floor when hunting.

Large front paws can kill small prey with one swipe. They also help the jaguar to swim.

Powerful jaws can pierce a skull or a turtle's shell.

Glossary

adaptation body part or behavior of a living thing that helps it survive in a particular habitat

apex predator animal that hunts other animals for food and is not hunted by any other animals for food

binocular vision using both eyes together to see

camera trap hidden camera that takes pictures of animals in the wild

camouflage blending in with the environment to hide

classify group living things together by their similarities and differences

consumer animal that eats plants or other animals

crepuscular active in the early morning and early evening

feces poop

food chain sequence in which one creature eats another, which eats another, and so on

food web network of intertwined food chains

genes characteristics passed on from a parent to offspring

groom clean an animal's fur

habitat type of place or surroundings that a living thing prefers to live in

home range area in which an animal usually lives

instinct natural tendency or way of behaving

litter group of young animals born at the same time

mate come together to reproduce or have young

melanistic condition where animals have black fur rather than typical coloring

opportunistic able to hunt and kill whatever prey is available

pregnant condition where a female animal is carrying developing young in her body

prey animal that is hunted and killed for food by another animal

producer plant in a food chain that makes food

reproduce to have offspring

rosette spotted pattern on a jaguar's fur

scent-marking marking territory using smell

species group of similar living things that can mate with each other

tactile to do with the sense of touch

territorial when an animal claims an area of land as its own space

trophy something to show an achievement, for example some hunters kill animals to show their skill

urine liquid waste from an animal

Find Out More

Books

Cox, Michael. *Big Cats*. New York: Bloomsbury Publishing, 2012.

Gagne, Tammy. *Cheetahs*. Mankato, Minn.: Capstone Press, 2012.

Ganeri, Anita. *South America's Most Amazing Animals*. Chicago: Raintree, 2008.

Websites

BBC Nature

www.bbc.co.uk/nature/life/Jaguar

Visit this website to watch videos of jaguars in the wild.

The Jaguar Conservation Fund

www.jaguar.org.br/en/index.html

Visit this website to see what work is being done to protect jaguars in Brazil.

Organizations

The World Wildlife Fund

www.wwf.org

WWF works to protect animals and nature, and needs your help! Take a look at their website and see what you can do.

The Born Free Foundation

www.bornfree.org

This charity works to protect cheetahs and many other endangered wild animals.

Panthera

www.panthera.org

This leading charity that works to protect jaguars and other big cats. Find out more about their work on their website.

Index